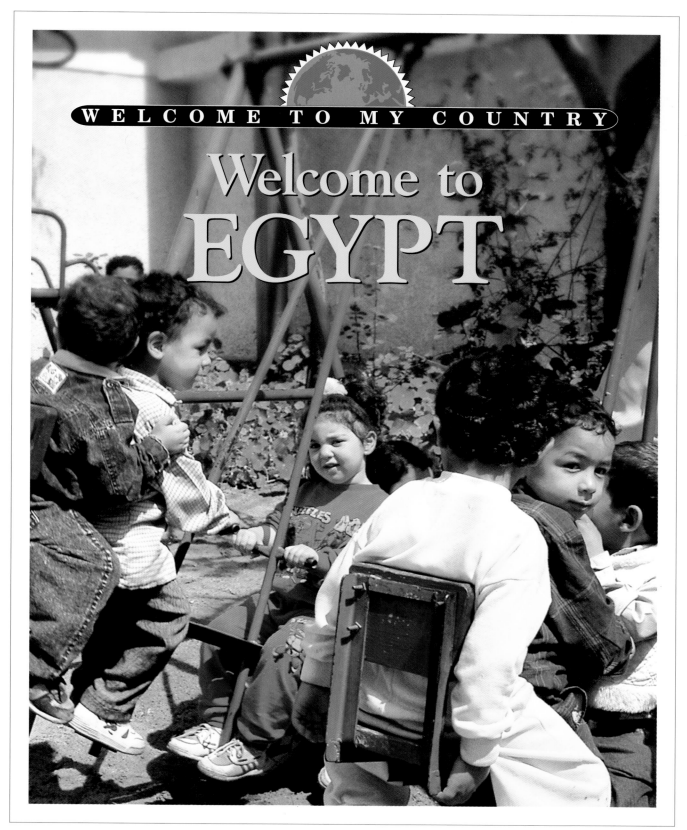

WELCOME TO MY COUNTRY

Welcome to
EGYPT

Gareth Stevens Publishing
MILWAUKEE

Written by
NICOLE FRANK/SUSAN L. WILSON

Designed by
JAILANI BASARI

Picture research by
SUSAN JANE MANUEL

First published in North America in 2000 by
Gareth Stevens Publishing
1555 North RiverCenter Drive, Suite 201
Milwaukee, Wisconsin 53212 USA

For a free color catalog describing
Gareth Stevens' list of high-quality books
and multimedia programs, call
1-800-542-2595 (USA) or
1-800-461-9120 (CANADA).
Gareth Stevens Publishing's
Fax: (414) 225-0377.

All rights reserved. No parts of this book may be reproduced or
utilized in any form or by any means electronic or mechanical,
including photocopying, recording, or by an information storage and
retrieval system, without permission from the copyright owner.

© **TIMES EDITIONS PTE LTD 2000**
Originated and designed by
Times Editions Pte Ltd
Times Centre, 1 New Industrial Road
Singapore 536196
http://www.timesone.com.sg/te

Library of Congress Cataloging-in-Publication Data
available upon request from the publisher.
Fax: (414) 225-0377 for the attention of the
Publishing Records Department.

ISBN 0-8368-2494-6

PICTURE CREDITS
Kristie Burns: 24, 25, 27, 33 (both), 34,
    38, 39
Bruce Coleman Collection: 3 (top), 9, 14
Focus Team Photo Agency: 7, 8 (bottom), 43
Itamar Grinberg: 4
Haga Library: 22, 23
The Hutchison Library: 19 (bottom)
The Image Bank: 18, 28
International Photobank: 30
Jason Lauré: 12
Christine Osborne Pictures: 1, 5 (center),
    17, 19 (top), 41
Still Pictures: 3 (center), 20
Liba Taylor Photography: cover, 3 (bottom),
    35, 37
Tan Chung Lee: 40
Topham Picturepoint: 2, 5, 6, 10, 13,
    15 (both), 21, 29, 31, 32, 36
Travel Ink: 11
Trip Photographic Library: 16, 26, 45
Nik Wheeler: 8 (top)

Digital Scanning by Superskill Graphics Pte Ltd

Printed in Malaysia

1 2 3 4 5 6 7 8 9 04 03 02 01 00

Contents

Words that appear in the glossary are printed in **boldface** type the first time they occur in the text.

4

Welcome to Egypt!

Egypt is a land of pyramids, temples, and mummies — powerful reminders of its ancient past. Present-day Egypt, however, has undergone many changes since the days of the king-gods. Let's meet the Egyptians and find out more about the "Land of the Pharaohs."

Opposite: The Temple of Karnak in Luxor was built about four thousand years ago.

Below: The children of Egypt welcome you: *ahlan wa sahlan* (AH-lan was-AH-lan)!

The Flag of Egypt

Egypt's flag was adopted in 1952. The color red represents **revolution**, white a bright future, and black a dark past. In the center of the flag is a golden eagle.

5

The Land

Located in the northeastern corner of Africa, Egypt covers 386,562 square miles (1,001,455 square kilometers). It connects Africa with Asia and Europe. The capital of Egypt is Cairo.

Most of Egypt consists of desert. The Nile River divides the country into the Eastern and Western Deserts. The

Below: Egypt's Western Desert is part of the Sahara Desert, which covers much of northern Africa.

Western Desert contains bare rocks and almost no vegetation. Mountains border the Eastern Desert along the Red Sea coast. The Sinai Peninsula of Egypt is also a desert.

Above: The Red Sea is filled with many kinds of marine life, including more than one thousand species of fish!

The Nile River flows from central Africa and empties into the Mediterranean Sea. At 4,131 miles (6,648 kilometers) in length, it is the world's longest river. Each year, heavy rains cause the Nile to overflow its banks. Dams help control these floods.

7

Seasons

Egypt has only two seasons. During the hot season from May to October, desert temperatures can reach 126° Fahrenheit (52° Celsius). The cool season lasts from November to April, with temperatures of about 55° to 70° F (13° to 21° C).

Above: Date palm trees grow throughout Egypt.

Left: Egypt receives very little rainfall. **Barren** mountains cover much of the land along the Red Sea and the Nile River.

Plants and Animals

Despite its dry climate, Egypt is home to abundant wildlife, including camels, horses, water buffalo, snakes, lizards, rats, bats, and mice. Every winter, more than one million birds fly through Egypt on their journey from Europe. Egyptian law protects rare species, such as cranes and herons.

The Nile River valley, the **delta**, and the **oases** support lotus and papyrus plants. The ancient Egyptians used papyrus stems to make paper.

Left: The Egyptian cobra grows to a length of about 6 feet (1.8 meters). It eats birds and toads.

History

Egypt's earliest inhabitants lived more than 250,000 years ago. In about 25,000 B.C., Egypt's climate changed, and its grassy plains became deserts. By 3400 B.C., groups of farmers were building the first settlements in Egypt.

Left: The Sphinx guards the Great Pyramids. This huge monument has the face of a man and the body of a lion.

Above: The pyramid of Khufu attracts thousands of tourists every year.

In the period 3400 to 3100 B.C., **pharaohs** (FAIR-ohs) began to rule Egypt. Pharaoh Menes (MEE-neez) united northern and southern Egypt. A succession of thirty **dynasties** ruled Egypt until Greek ruler Alexander the Great invaded in 330 B.C. About six hundred years later, the Romans defeated Egypt's Queen Cleopatra VII, making Egypt part of the Roman Empire.

In A.D. 639, the Arabs invaded Egypt, introducing the Islamic religion. In the 1500s, Egypt became part of the Turkish Ottoman Empire.

Modern History

The British controlled Egypt from the late 1700s to the twentieth century. Egypt gained partial independence from Britain in 1922. Egyptian **nationalists** formed an organization called the Wafd (WAH-fed) to fight for Egypt's full independence. This was not achieved, however, until 1952, when Egyptian leader Gamal Abdel Nasser led a successful revolution against British rule. In 1954, Nasser became president of Egypt.

Below: A parade of Egyptian troops celebrates victory in the 1973 war against Israel.

Above: Egyptian President Hosni Mubarak (*right*) meets with Syrian leader Farouk al Sharaa (*left*) and Saudi Arabian leader Al Faisal (*center*) to foster good relations between their countries.

After Nasser died in 1970, Anwar al-Sadat became president. In 1978, war broke out between Israel and its Arab neighbors, and Sadat negotiated for peace. After talks held at Camp David in the United States, a peace treaty was signed in 1979. In 1981, Sadat was killed by **assassins** from secret groups that wanted to make Egypt a pure Islamic society.

Hosni Mubarak then became Egypt's president. He has continued to work for peace in the Middle East.

Ramses II (Nineteenth Dynasty)

Pharaoh Ramses II ruled Egypt from 1304 B.C. to 1237 B.C. He competed with other rulers to build the grandest temples for the Egyptian god Amun.

Above: This giant monument, the head of Ramses II, is located in Luxor. Luxor was once known as Thebes.

Queen Hatshepsut (Eighteenth Dynasty)

Queen Hatshepsut made herself pharaoh after her husband, Pharaoh Thutmosis II, died. She ruled Egypt from about 1503 B.C. to 1482 B.C.

Above: President Gamal Abdel Nasser attempted to forge an alliance of all Arab nations.

Gamal Abdel Nasser (1918–1970)

In 1952, Gamal Abdel Nasser helped launch the revolution to overthrow British rule in Egypt. Two years later, he became Egypt's president. Nasser **reformed** the new nation's economy along **socialist** lines.

Anwar al-Sadat (1918–1981)

As president, Muhammad Anwar al-Sadat helped secure peace between Egypt and Israel. He also improved relations between Egypt and the U.S. by ending Nasser's socialist system of government.

Above: In 1978, President Anwar al-Sadat received the Nobel Peace Prize for his role in improving Egypt-Israeli relations.

Government and the Economy

Egypt is a **democratic republic** ruled by a president. Muhammad Hosni Mubarak, the current president, has been in office since 1981.

Egypt's government consists of three branches — **legislative**, **executive**, and **judicial** — plus the Shura Consultative Council. The legislative branch, called the People's Assembly, makes laws and approves state policy. In 1998, the People's Assembly had 454 members.

Below: Egyptians line up to vote. Egypt's system of government supports many political parties.

Executive power lies with the president, who is **nominated** by the People's Assembly and elected by the public. The president appoints cabinet ministers and the prime minister, who heads the government.

Judicial matters are decided by judges in a system of courts. The Shura Consultative Council advises the government but has no real authority. Eighty-eight of its 264 members are appointed by the president.

Above: The government helps provide the poor with health care, education, and child care.

Economy

In 1997, the average Egyptian earned about $1,100 a year. The large group of poor people in Egypt are called *fellahin* (FELL-ah-heen). About 40 percent of Egyptians work on farms, 30 percent in government jobs, and 20 percent in private businesses. About 8–11 percent are unemployed.

Left: Egypt's capital, Cairo, is a growing city, where many business meetings take place.

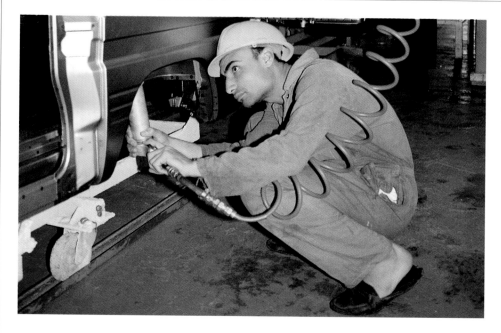

Left: Egypt has a shortage of good jobs. Many skilled people work in jobs that do not require their particular skills.

Cotton, petroleum, and aluminum products are Egypt's biggest exports. Imported products include flour, meat, cars, and steel.

Tourism plays an important role in Egypt's economy. Every year, thousands of people visit Egypt to marvel at its ancient treasures.

Below: Oil is Egypt's most valuable mineral resource.

The Suez Canal

Connecting the Mediterranean Sea with the Red Sea, the Suez Canal is one of the world's busiest shipping routes and a major source of Egypt's income.

People and Lifestyle

Although their ancestors might be **Nubian** (NOO-be-an), **Bedouin** (BED-oo-in), Arabic, Greek, Italian, Syrian, or Lebanese, most modern Egyptians simply think of themselves as Egyptian.

Social class, established by birth or cultural background (not income or skin color), determines a person's position in life.

Left: Fellahin children ride to market. More than half of all Egyptians live in rural areas.

Left: Most Bedouins live in the Sinai Peninsula.

The Nubians came from ancient Nubia in Sudan. They fished and farmed along the Nile River until the 1960s, when the Aswan High Dam was built, flooding the land.

The Bedouins do not set up permanent homes but move in search of pasture for their sheep and camel herds. However, some Bedouins have settled on the Mediterranean coast. Others are still **nomadic**.

Family Life

In Egyptian families, boys and girls have different roles. Girls help their mothers at home, while boys work and play with other boys and men.

Later in life, men are seen as the source of income for their families. They are expected to have a job and earn a living. Women are responsible for taking care of the children and the household.

Above: Family outings are a fun way to spend the day. Girls and boys talk and play in separate groups.

Unlike children in the West, Egyptian boys and girls do not "date." A girl must be at least sixteen and a boy eighteen to be married.

Egyptians regard marriage and the birth of children as life's happiest events. Many marriages are arranged. Getting married involves two parts — signing the marriage contract and announcing the marriage to the public.

Below: Families visit the graves of their loved ones on *Eid el-Adha* (EYE-eed el-AD-hah), the festival of the big feast.

Education

Just over half of all Egyptians over the age of fifteen can read and write. The Egyptian government is trying to raise this rate and prepare citizens for the challenges of the future.

Formal education for children begins at the age of five. Although primary school education is required, many poor families do not send all their children to school. Instead, they rely on

Below: Carpet weaving is a suitable trade for girls with small, quick fingers.

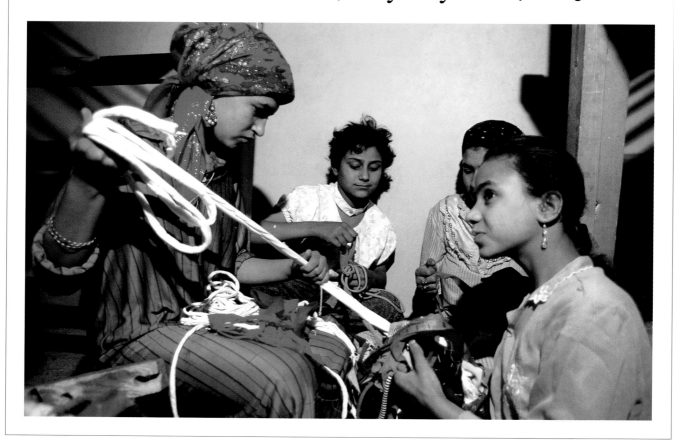

Left: Egyptian schoolchildren learn Arabic. The Arabic alphabet has twenty-eight letters and fourteen symbols.

the children to earn money or help out in family businesses. Three years of preparatory school follow primary school. Then, based on their exam results, students go either to a general school that prepares them for a university or to a specialized school that trains them for a technical job. University education is free for those who pass the entrance exams, but many students work instead, to earn a living.

Left: The mosque of Muhammad 'Ali is a monument to Muhammad 'Ali Pasha, ruler of Egypt in the early nineteenth century.

Religion

About 84 percent of Egyptians are Muslim. They practice Islam, the national religion of Egypt. Fifteen percent of the population is Christian.

Islam is not just a religion but an entire way of life, combining religion with culture and moral values. Muslims worship Allah, or God. The Qur'an (KOUR-aan), or Koran, is the Muslim holy book.

Christianity reached Egypt very early, probably during the time of the Apostles. Most Egyptian Christians belong to the Coptic Christian Church, which claims St. Mark, the author of the second Gospel, as its founder. From A.D. 312 until the Arabs invaded Egypt in the seventh century, Christianity was the national religion of Egypt. Today, the Coptic Christians, or Copts, are a successful community in Egypt.

Below: Egyptian children take a walk with a Christian nun. Copt schools in Egypt are open to Muslims, too.

Language

Until the seventh century, Coptic was Egypt's official language. Since then, Arabic has been the national language. Today, both Copts and Muslims speak Arabic.

Arabic has many different **dialects**. Most Arabic speakers understand Egyptian **Colloquial** Arabic (the informal, everyday form of the language) because Egyptian film, television, and newspapers use it. The Qur'an is written in classical Arabic.

Below: Ancient Egyptians wrote in **hieroglyphics** — a kind of picture script. Hieroglyphic symbols were often carved on rocks or temple walls.

Left: Najib Mahfouz's *Cairo Trilogy* — *Palace Walk*, *Palace of Desire*, and *Sugar Street* — won him the Nobel Prize for Literature in 1988.

Arabic is written from right to left. Some styles of Arabic writing are truly beautiful — *calligraphy* is the Arabic word for "the art of handwriting."

Many Egyptian novels and plays focus on Islamic history and Western influence. Egypt's noted authors include Najib Mahfouz, Taha Husayn, Mahmud Taymur, and Abbas al-Aqqad.

Arts

Egypt abounds with artistic treasure, both old and new. The ancient Egyptians expressed their religious experiences through painting, sculpture, and **relief**. Ancient Egyptian art shows human figures in perfect form — young, beautiful, and powerful. The artists intentionally avoided depicting old age and illness.

Left: The temple of Ramses II stands in Abu Simbel, near Aswan. Ramses II was Egypt's longest reigning pharaoh.

Ancient Egyptian works of art tell a story. Two types of paintings and reliefs decorate the walls of temples and tombs — formal scenes and

depictions of ordinary life. Found mainly in temples, formal scenes show the world of royalty, the gods, and the dead. Tombs feature scenes of daily life — fishing and farming activities. In both kinds of scenes, the bigger the figure, the more important he or she was.

Above: The tomb of King Tutankhamun, or "King Tut," contains many beautiful and priceless objects.

Left: Unlike the pharaohs before him, Pharaoh Akhenaten and his wife, Nefertiti, worshiped only one God, named Aten. Aten is represented by the golden sphere above the figures' heads.

Sculpture and Relief

Sculpture was an early development in Egyptian art. Sculpted works featured pharaohs, queens, and other members of the royal family.

The ancient Egyptians favored two types of relief — bas-relief, where the background was cut away; and sunken relief, where figures were carved into the stone.

The Pharos Lighthouse (which is now gone) at Alexandria and the Great Pyramids at Giza rank among the Seven Wonders of the Ancient World. The pyramids are still regarded as an amazing architectural achievement.

Above: Composer George Kazazian plays the lute.

Left: This boy engraves a brass plate. Egyptians have always excelled at crafts and folk art, including pottery, embroidery, and metal engraving.

Leisure

Most Egyptians enjoy spending time with family and friends. Many city dwellers live in the same neighborhoods as their relatives and close friends and visit them often.

Women tend to meet in the home, but groups often gather outdoors to talk and offer each other support, as they go about their busy days.

Below: Many families celebrate holidays at the beach.

Left: Egyptian children go for a donkey ride.

Women take charge of bringing up the children and teaching them moral values and cultural and religious traditions. Folk tales illustrate the difference between right and wrong and the importance of good friendships.

Men spend more of their leisure time in public places than women. Many men play board games at local cafés in the evening.

At night, the streets of Cairo are busy with people walking, shopping, or eating at streetside stalls and cafés.

Sports

Egyptians enjoy polo, squash, basketball, swimming, and handball, but the most popular sport is soccer (called football). Soccer fans watch the sport on television or attend games at the Cairo National Stadium or Military Academy Stadium.

Egyptian schools do not have organized sporting events. Instead, these events are sponsored by private

Below: Boys play soccer in front of the pyramids.

Left: Wealthy Egyptians lawn bowl at a private club in Cairo.

sports clubs. Most sporting events are too expensive for the average Egyptian to attend.

The two top soccer teams in Egypt are the al-Ahly Club and the Zamalek Club. Both are based in Cairo, and each has an impressive record of cup wins and league championships.

In 1996, Egypt hosted the al-Ahram International Squash Tournament. Participants competed in various events ranging from athletics to horse racing.

Major Holidays and Festivals

Muslims celebrate three major festivals: *Moulid el-Nabi* (MOO-led el-NAH-bi), *Eid el-Adha*, and *Eid el-Fitr* (EYE-eed el-FIT-er).

Moulid el-Nabi marks the birth of the Prophet Muhammad, the founder of Islam. Homes are decorated, and festivities take place in open tents. Wealthier families may go to a mosque in Cairo to celebrate the holiday, while others have a big meal at home. During

Below: Sufis, an order of Muslims, connect with God through dance.

the celebrations, merchants sell brightly colored candy dolls that symbolize the Prophet's birthday.

Above: Schoolchildren practice for a musical they will perform during Ramadan.

Eid el-Adha (the big feast) takes place after the annual **pilgrimage** to Mecca, the Islamic holy place in Saudi Arabia.

Eid el-Fitr (the little feast) celebrates the end of Ramadan (RA-ma-DAAN), the ninth month of the Islamic calendar. During Ramadan, Muslims fast throughout the day, eating only after sunset.

Food

Except for a few distinctly Egyptian dishes, most food in Egypt is a mix of Turkish, Greek, Palestinian, Lebanese, and Syrian **cuisine**.

Basic Foods and Main Meals

Bread, *foul* (FOOL), and *ta'miya* (ta-MEE-ya) are the basic foods in an Egyptian diet. Like pita bread, Egyptian bread is flat. Foul is boiled

Below: This woman is baking flat, pita-like bread. You can make a pocket in the bread and fill it with all kinds of tasty ingredients.

Left: Bread, chickpeas, and fava beans are the basic foods in the Egyptian diet.

fava beans. Ta'miya, also called *felafel* (fey-LAH-fel), are fried balls of chickpeas and wheat.

Lunch is the main meal of the day, while dinner is smaller and simpler. Desserts consist of puddings and sweet cakes.

All Egyptians, even poor families, welcome their guests with generous meals. To be considered a good guest in Egypt, you must eat a lot!

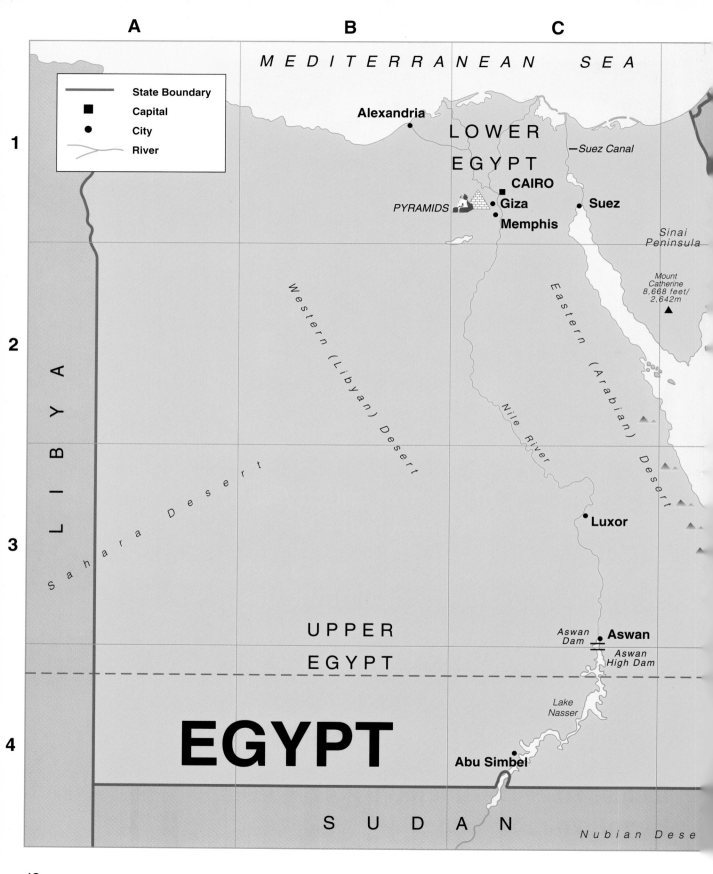

MEDITERRANEAN SEA

A **B** **C**

Alexandria

L O W E R
E G Y P T

—*Suez Canal*

CAIRO

PYRAMIDS • **Giza**
• **Suez**
• **Memphis**

*Sinai
Peninsula*

*Mount
Catherine
8,668 feet/
2,642m* ▲

State Boundary
Capital
City
River

1

2

Western (Libyan) Desert

Eastern (Arabian) Desert

Nile River

S a h a r a   D e s e r t

L I B Y A

• **Luxor**

3

U P P E R

E G Y P T

*Aswan
Dam* • **Aswan**

*Aswan
High Dam*

*Lake
Nasser*

EGYPT

4

Abu Simbel •

S U D A N

Nubian Dese

42

Above: As part of the sound and light show at Giza, the Sphinx tells the story of the Great Pyramids.

Abu Simbel C4
Alexandria B1
Aswan C3
Aswan Dam C3
Aswan High Dam C3

Cairo C1

Eastern Desert C2

Giza C1

Israel D1

Jordan D1

Libya A1–A4
Lower Egypt B1–B2
Luxor C3

Mediterranean Sea
    B1–C1
Memphis C1
Mount Catherine D2

Nasser, Lake C4
Nile River C2–C3
Nubian Desert
    C4–D4

Pyramids C1

Red Sea D3

Sahara Desert A3
Saudi Arabia D2

Sinai Peninsula
    C1–D1
Sudan B4
Suez C1
Suez Canal C1

Upper Egypt B3–B4

West Bank D1
Western Desert B2

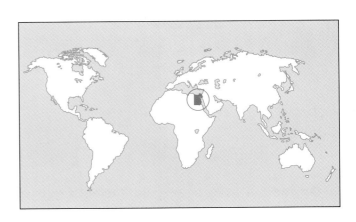

Quick Facts

Official Name   Arab Republic of Egypt; Jumhuriyah Misr al-Arabiyah

Capital   Cairo

Official Language   Arabic

Population   63.6 million

Land Area   386,562 square miles (1,001,455 sq. km)

Divisions   26 governorates

Highest Point   Mount Catherine (Jabal Katrina): 8,668 feet (2,642 m)

Major River   Nile

Main Religion   Islam

Flag   Three equal horizontal bands of red (top), white (center), and black (bottom), with the national emblem, an eagle, centered in the white band

Government   Republic

Head of State   President (Muhammad Hosni Mubarak, elected in 1981)

National Holiday   Anniversary of the Revolution, July 23

Currency   Egyptian pound (3.4 pounds = U.S. $1 in 1999)

 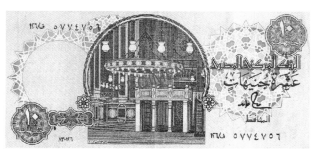

Opposite: Actors recreate ancient Egypt at Dr. Ragab's Pharaonic Village near Cairo.

Glossary

assassins: people who murder a politically important person.

barren: infertile; not capable of supporting vegetation.

Bedouin (BED-oo-in)**:** a nomadic Arab living in Egypt, North Africa, or the Arabian Peninsula.

colloquial: informal, ordinary.

cuisine: food.

delta: a flat plain at a river's mouth.

democratic: relating to a system of government in which supreme power rests with the people.

dialects: regional varieties of a certain language.

dynasties: families of rulers.

executive: relating to the administrative or governing authority.

fellahin (FELL-ah-heen)**:** the poor class in Egypt.

hieroglyphics: a picture script used by ancient Egyptians.

judicial: relating to the enforcing of justice by courts of law.

legislative: relating to the law and the making of laws.

nationalists: people who are devoted and loyal to their country.

nomadic: relating to people who do not set up permanent homes but move from place to place in search of pasture for their cattle.

nominated: proposed for an appointment or position.

Nubian (NOO-be-an)**:** a dark-skinned Egyptian from the southern part of the country.

oases: fertile areas in a desert region, usually having a spring or some other source of water.

pharaohs: Egyptian kings.

pilgrimage: a religious journey.

reformed: changed.

relief: a form of sculpture in which figures are carved to project, or stand out, from the background.

republic: a nation in which supreme power rests with the people, who elect their representatives to govern.

revolution: the overthrow of the government that is in power.

socialist: a system of government in which the state owns all businesses.

More Books To Read

Ancient Egyptian Places. People and Places series. Sarah McNeill and Sarah Howarth (Millbrook Press)

Cleopatra. First Book series. Robert Green (Franklin Watts)

The Curse of Tutankhamen. Mysteries of Science series. Elaine Landau (Millbrook Press)

Egypt. Country Fact Files series. Emma Loveridge (Raintree/ Steck Vaughn)

Egypt. Enchantment of the World second series. Ann Heinrichs (Children's Press)

Egypt. Major World Nations series. Frances Wilkins and Frances Wilkens (Chelsea House)

Egypt. On the Map series. David Flint (Raintree/Steck Vaughn)

The Great Pyramid. Wonders of the World series. Elizabeth Mann (Mikaya Press)

Science in Ancient Egypt. First Book series. Geraldine Woods (Franklin Watts)

The Valley of the Kings. Digging up the Past series. Peter A. Clayton (Thomas Learning)

Videos

Egypt. (Education 2000)

Egypt — Secrets of the Pharaohs. (National Geographic)

The Great Pharaohs of Egypt. (A & E Entertainment)

Sphinx of Egypt. (A & E)

Web Sites

touregypt.net/wildegypt/

www.seaworld.org/Egypt/egypt.html

www.globalfriends.com/html/ world_tour/egypt/egypt.htm

Due to the dynamic nature of the Internet, some web sites stay current longer than others. To find additional web sites, use a reliable search engine with one or more of the following keywords to help you locate information on Egypt. Keywords: *Bedouins, Cairo, Egyptians, Nubians, pyramids, Ramses II, Sphinx, Suez Canal.*

Index